# THE SERPENT WITHIN

*Navigating Fear to Restore Inner Harmony*

# Also by Roddy Carter

*BodyWHealth: Journey to Abundance*

*Sunset Lessons: Reflections on Light and Love
from the Darkest of Places*

*Fireside Wisdom: Conversations to Inspire Personal Mastery*

*The Problem With Anger: And How to Solve It*

*Becoming Unstoppable: Your Neurocentric Coaching Guide to Achieving
Unstoppable Success*

*Unstoppable You* Online Courses
(available from www.roddycarter.com):
*Unstoppable You*
*Unstoppable You Business*
*Unleash Unstoppable*
*Unleash Success*

# THE SERPENT WITHIN

*Navigating Fear to
Restore Inner Harmony*

Roddy Carter, MD

Aquila Life Science Press
La Jolla, California

FIRST AQUILA LIFE SCIENCE PRESS EDITION, JANUARY 2025
Published by Aquila Life Science, LLC, La Jolla, CA

THE PROBLEM WITH ANGER.

Copyright © 2025 by Aquila Life Science, LLC.
Illustration by Rebecca Myers.
Editing and book design by Sarah Dawson, WordPlay Editing.

All rights reserved.

No part of this publication may be reproduced, stored in a retrieval system, or transmitted in any form or by any means, electronic, mechanical, photocopying, recording, scanning, or otherwise, except as permitted under Section 107 or 108 of the 1976 United States Copyright Act, without the prior written permission of the Publisher. Any request to the Publisher for permission should be sent to Aquila Life Science, LLC, at connect@aquilalifescience.com.

Limit of Liability/Disclaimer of Warranty: While the publisher and author have used their best effort in preparing this book, they make no representations or warranties with respect to the accuracy or completeness of the contents of this book and specifically disclaim any implied warranties of merchantability or fitness for a particular purpose. No warranty may be created or extended by sales representatives or written sales materials. Some materials included with standard print versions of this book may not be included in the e-book or audiobook version.

ISBN: 979-8-9895751-5-2

*Printed in the United States of America*

*To all who have felt a pain within*

*and, not knowing its origin or meaning,*

*have toiled in silent suffering.*

# ACKNOWLEDGEMENTS

I am deeply grateful to Sarah Dawson, whose editorial excellence continues to elevate my work. With an exceptional ability, Sarah deftly enhances my voice, balancing empathy with precision. Her keen eye for both the broader narrative and the finest detail helps the story flow seamlessly, ensuring we ultimately deliver accessible, engaging prose. Sarah, thank you for your meaningful contribution to my work; your talent and dedication help me to breathe life into words.

I would also like to express my appreciation to Rebecca Myers, whose artistic interpretation has brought this parable to life through her beautiful, rich illustrations. Rebecca's sensitive ear and loyal creativity add layers of meaning, inviting readers to see and feel the narrative in ways that words alone cannot achieve.

# PREFACE

I love telling stories.

To me, storytelling is both an art and a teaching tool. I've used it often throughout my career to make complex science accessible to everyone. In my role as an executive coach, I frequently use stories to translate abstract neuroscience into actionable insights.

Through the power of imagination, I have seen many people come to understand the workings of their own brains, enabling them to seize back authority over that most magnificent organ, which is their greatest gift. Consequently, they have invited peace and joy into their lives and have achieved the success that they so richly deserve.

In this book, I want to share the same gift with you. I begin with a parable, a tale about one Sage's quest for wisdom. Then, I explain the science behind the story, giving you the knowledge you need to transform your life.

So, take a deep breath and prepare to enter the theatre of your imagination, joining the Sage on his powerful journey.

# CHAPTER 1

## THE SAGE

He left as the sun set, and would be back before it rose again. This journey was no secret, really, but he chose to do it alone. He needed his physical strength for the arduous trip, his intellectual strength for the challenging conversations ahead, and his emotional strength for it all.

The villagers would no doubt be surprised by his mission. He was highly respected, even adored. They believed there were no bounds to his knowledge and wisdom.

His home was in the center of the village, both physically and spiritually. All the roads and paths began there and radiated outward toward the sprawling, growing periphery. Or, looked at another way, all the roads and paths led to his door.

The villagers brought him all their troubles, disputes, and joys. He was their guide, their counselor, their educator, and their healer, trained by the great leaders who had preceded him.

And so, they would be surprised to know that this time it was he who was seeking guidance.

He had become aware of the insidious change several years prior. Slowly, almost imperceptibly, the peace and harmony that had warmly enswathed every home and gathering place began to shift. Discord silently wound its way through the village.

He'd watched as arguments broke out between neighbors. Husbands and wives began quarreling. Siblings disputed ownership of the scanty belongings of deceased parents. Merchants complained that townspeople no longer valued their goods. Laborers argued with employers about wages. Landlords evicted their tenants.

Each escalating controversy could be traced back to a minor disagreement between villagers who initially pursued their dispute quietly and respectfully. But over time, harsh words and unkindness crept in. He knew this because, when each conflict was at its ugliest, they brought it to him for arbitration.

## The Sage

"Arbitration"? Even this was a new word in the village. The concept had not existed in this loving and peaceful community before now.

He always did his best to judge with kindness and fairness. He weighed each decision with empathy, striving for an equitable outcome for both parties that reflected the integrity of the village and its legacy. The process was exhausting, though, especially now that he too was entrapped in the odious malady of strife.

It had happened one evening over dinner. Tired of their bickering, he had snapped at his two oldest children—both grown men—with uncharacteristic venom in his words.

The sons grimaced in obvious pain, as though stabbed by the ceremonial sword that would be their inheritance. Their wives and sisters looked stunned. His grandchildren, previously running and playing loudly, fell silent. A tear ran down his wife's cheek.

He, too, had succumbed.

*****

Following that incident, he stayed secluded in his home for several days, sitting in his leather chair, gazing up at the mountain, looking for answers. He had spent many fitful nights worrying about the epidemic of disharmony and discord gripping his village, but it was different now that he, too, had become ensnared.

Finally, he decided that he must journey to visit her. He could only solve the problem with the help of her beauty and wisdom.

The sun cast pink streaks across the western sky as he tied the straps of his sturdy walking sandals. The days were warm, but the nights were cold. Long shadows coalesced into an overwhelming darkness both literally and figuratively, so he carried his heavy cloak with him in a canvas bag. He would need it at the top of the mountain when the heavens sucked the warmth of the earth from beneath his feet.

While he walked, he thought of nothing.

He consciously emptied his mind. He knew he would need all his intellectual power if he were to see the world with fresh eyes. With each step, he journeyed closer to untouched nature. His mind settled gradually into the rhythm of the universe. He reached the top physically drained but mentally ready.

He crested the last steep pathway, eager to cast his eyes on her. She was not there yet, but he was not concerned. He knew she would come. He found a spot with large boulders and sat with his back to them to shelter him from the cold breeze that came off the ocean in the west. And he waited. He might have dozed; he couldn't be sure.

The light shifted, almost imperceptibly—the first hint of her arrival.

He raised his eyes in eager anticipation. He almost stood. He wanted to run to greet her but knew that would be futile. He must wait patiently. Royalty is not hurried. She would travel to him with serene grace, at her own pace.

He felt the darkness lifting. After a short wait, he could see her full, beautiful face. He could discern every line and contour, each a testament to her wisdom. At times he had to look away, her beauty blinding. He waited in awe. She would speak when she was ready.

He used the time to hold all the details of his vexing challenge in the forefront of his mind. This journey was for his people; he wanted to help them restore tranquility to the village. He knew he must first understand what it was that had afflicted them.

Suddenly, he heard her gentle voice.

"You are a great physician. You have been trained by your mother, and her father and grandfather. Before them, your

# The Sage

great-great grandmother learned what it meant to be human. You have succumbed to your human frailty. You have earnestly sought understanding. You have spent days and nights combing through your knowledge of the heart to find a solution. You have failed. Perhaps you are looking in the wrong place?"

Her words penetrated his senses like the sharply defined outlines of the trees he had watched silhouetted against the setting sun.

A problem this big could only start in one of two places.

He had spent his time thinking about the most obvious: His heart was heavy, as were those of his people. Surely that must be where the malice had taken up residence—in their hearts? And yet, she had disagreed.

Without hesitation, he began to think about the only other place it could be: their minds.

He spent time considering how the products of the mind—thoughts, feelings, and fears—each jockeyed for control of the human to whom they belonged, a delicate struggle for leadership and balance. He wondered what significance each one played in the chaos of his village. These musings consumed him as she slipped away into the darkness.

He was angry with himself for not noticing her departure. He knew that she had guided him closer to the answer, but he still could not see it clearly. He would need to return the next evening to learn more.

*****

The day passed rapidly. He was excited to return to the mountaintop in the evening, to see her again, to hear her voice, and to resume his quest, guided by her wisdom and light.

His hike down the mountain had been almost effortless the night before as he thought about their conversation. Her question

## The Sage

echoed in his mind throughout the day. He remained sequestered in his home, deep in contemplative isolation.

The villagers began to worry. They had not seen their leader in days now, and tempers were becoming frayed. Violence erupted sporadically as frustration leeched into everyday life. Chaos erupted briefly when an elderly woman set fire to her neighbor's house after a seemingly trivial altercation.

None of this brought the leader out of his seclusion. He knew that the solution was within. His crusade became more urgent.

He could see the dying embers of the house fire in the distance as he climbed the mountain the second night. White smoke slithered sinuously up into the darkness.

As he turned the final bend to the top of the mountain, he was startled by a sudden movement in the path ahead. In the dark, he could just see the quick thrust of a striking snake—one he knew to be poisonous, whose venom could kill a grown man in mere hours. He jumped into the dirt on the side of the path, rolling clumsily before stopping against a large rock. He hurt from the fall but knew he was lucky to have evaded a fatal attack.

As he made his careful way back to the path, his mind raced forward to his meeting. In his eager anticipation, her image filled his heart, and he quickly forgot about the lucky escape as he crested the mountain, this time undisturbed by any other creature.

Again, she was not yet there. Again, he found a sheltered recess in the windswept plateau. Again, he rested, trusting in her imminent arrival.

He saw her as she slid silently over the horizon. The top of her head glowed white. He knew that he would soon see her whole face. He knew each contour and shadow, and eagerly awaited her full appearance. As always, she did not rush. As always, he waited patiently.

When he heard her gentle voice, she was so close he felt he could almost touch her.

"You have done well, wise leader. Last night you identified the source of your people's suffering. You will help your people, and you will heal yourself. But tonight, I have unwelcome tidings for you: Now that you have this malady within, it will never leave you."

He dropped his gaze. This was terrible news. He had wanted to drive the curse out, to rid himself and his village of its toxic presence, forever.

As if to reassure him, she spoke again. "Tonight you must understand the nature of this eternal ailment. I sent you a message to prepare you for this insight."

He sat in silence for a long time, hoping she would speak again. Repeatedly, he looked up at her face. She seemed to stare right back at him, never moving her gaze.

He walked through the entire day in his mind. What was the preparatory message? Whom had she sent to deliver it? He had not spoken with anybody for days, sitting in mute reflection. He absently rubbed at his hip and winced when he touched the spreading bruise inflicted by the rock that had stopped him from falling farther down the mountain. Suddenly, he realized who the messenger was: the snake.

He knew these poisonous reptiles well. They were common in the desert surrounding the village, and harmless unless threatened. If driven to fear for their safety, though, they would strike with the speed of lightning, burying their sharp fangs in the flesh of the one who had threatened them, inflicting mortal injury. Even great warriors had succumbed to the poison of these otherwise meek and lovely creatures.

Gradually, the message and the insight became clear to the Sage. Every major disagreement in the village started with a minor dispute between two previously harmonious individuals. They felt threatened by each other, and so their fear responded—just like the snake had.

These inner fears asserted their primal control over inflicted villagers, invoking instinctive reflexes to fight or flee. They dispatched their messengers to all parts of the body with disturbing news of imminent danger. The villagers' bodies responded, their pulses quickening, their focus narrowing, their guts tightening, and their survival instincts taking control.

And with nowhere to flee, they fought. Nasty words erupted out of their minds and mouths. In an iterative fashion, the words escalated to hostile actions as the fear of each villager strove to protect its owner.

Previously amicable people now looked around with suspicion, expecting the worst from their neighbors.

The poison spread like wildfire. Each day the serpent took control of new minds and hearts. One home at a time, it had slithered its way through the village, until finally it entered the heart and mind of the leader, erupting in triumph in the ugly tongue-lashing he had given his sons.

He looked up, but she was gone. His heart raced and his mind was filled simultaneously with shame and elation. Now he understood. She had led him to this healing insight.

Exhausted but hopeful, he rose to descend the mountain. This time he walked more carefully, prodding the dark shadows in the path with a stick before passing. He would not make the same mistake twice.

For the first time in many days, he slept. His wife sensed a shift and asked him to explain, but he held his silence. He was not ready. He understood the problem, but he needed the solution. He needed to prepare himself for his final ascent.

*****

# The Sage

The third evening, he again strapped on his sturdy walking sandals. He carefully folded his ceremonial robe into his canvas bag. He would honor his guide and teacher tonight with his finest clothes. She had helped him to find wisdom and healing.

As soon as the villagers were indoors, he strode out toward the base of the mountain. He pushed hard on the ascent, mindful of dark hollows in the pathway. He stopped halfway to rest briefly. Turning to look over his village, he noticed a strange calm. It was almost as if the villagers slept quietly for the first time in a long while.

He quickly brought his attention back to his journey and resumed his climb. The last few miles seemed to take forever. He could hardly contain his excitement. He knew she would be there again. He crested just in time. She had already started across the plateau toward his cathartic resting place. He collapsed, out of breath.

She soon emerged fully, serene and unhurried as usual.

He smiled up at her, wanting to burst into words of excitement and appreciation. But he was a leader, and remembered his manners. He waited patiently.

She took a long time tonight. He began to worry that she would never speak, that he would have to return empty-handed, without a solution.

Then her brilliant gaze seemed to move closer, and he heard her whisper.

"You have done well, wise Sage. You have understood the eternal ailment. You have identified the role of the serpent and the source of the problem. I am proud that you have not condemned the serpent. This way would be disastrous. You need the serpent, but you must learn that it has a time and place in your life. You understand that, when it is given free reign, chaos and ugliness ensue. And now, you are ready for the final answer—but I will not give it to you tonight."

## The Sage

His heart sank. He was so close. He had come here knowing that he must solve the problem before he descended one last time, to return to his troubled people. His heart was working closely with his mind, and his mission had become a burning desire—a desire so strong that he truly *believed* that he would have the answer tonight.

As he contemplated this miserable outcome, he heard her whisper even more softly than before.

"I will not give you the answer because I already gave you the answer long ago. You have a gift the serpent cannot match. You were given this gift so that you would rule with wisdom and love. The gift gives you power over the serpent." With that, she fell silent.

*****

Perplexed and exhausted, he struggled through the night, pushing to find the elusive solution to this vexing and destructive riddle.

Finally, the sun's rays whispered in the east. Darkness began to melt away. He looked around to see if she was still with him. He could only see a faint outline of her face as she descended in the west, her royal visit over. He watched her with deep love and admiration.

Loneliness tugged at his heart, as he understood that he would have to solve this last piece of the mystery alone. She had given him the inspiration, but not the solution.

"Think, old man, think," he muttered. "The answer is within you, she said. Both the serpent and the power are within."

Suddenly, he understood. The serpent lived within. It always had. It was a part of the mind that wanted to protect its owner from danger. But the serpent could be controlled by the loving and thinking parts of the same mind. Yes! That was it!

"*Think*, old man, *think!*" That was the answer.

## The Sage

He stood quickly, feeling suddenly younger. He had not slept at all that night, yet he was filled with new energy. Excited about getting back to the village to share his knowledge, he strapped on his sandals and gathered up the warm robe he had huddled under through the cold night.

As he ran down the mountain, his mind raced with excitement. Bursting through the door of his home, he woke his sleeping family. "I have news," he blurted out.

They assembled with curious looks.

He stood tall and proud as he spoke. He started with an apology—first to his sons, and then to the entire family. He, the custodian of kindness and order, had failed them. He had not recognized the serpent within until it was too late. He had stood by, puzzled, while it almost destroyed the village, even his own family.

After speaking with his household, he gathered all who lived in the village. He explained to them the dominance of thoughts, especially when empowered by affirming and uplifting feelings—how, together, they could overcome fear.

He taught them to be aware of the times and places fear would emerge. He taught them how fear was designed to protect them, but he didn't need to describe the suffering that prevailed when it ruled unchecked. Repeatedly, he highlighted the immense power of thought and its ability to tame the serpent. Then he outlined tasks they should all practice, to help them make sure thoughts—and *not* fears—would be in control.

He concluded with the passionate claim that reason and love would always conquer the serpent that is fear.

*****

That night, the village was calm.

Adults digested the enormous insight that their leader had shared with them. Many would take days to fully understand the liberating power of the message. Parents spoke with their children, teaching them about the magical forces of intellect and emotion. Spouses and friends had open, honest conversations, putting reason and compassion back in charge in their relationships.

Harmony returned.

Alone, the old man rose and walked to the edge of the village. He would not climb the mountain tonight, for there was no need for conversation. He simply came to its base in deep reverence and appreciation for her guidance, and for the enduring, healing truth she had revealed.

He watched patiently.

After a long wait, the moon rose quietly in the east. Her majesty again brought light and serenity to the dark night. He bowed deeply to honor her power and insight.

# The Sage

## CHAPTER 2

# THE SCIENCE

I hope that your journey alongside the Sage was illuminating. I hope that you entered your powerful imagination and walked alongside the protagonist in your own dusty sandals. I hope that you felt his pain, and the pain of the village. I hope that you were puzzled and frustrated with him at the sequential (but incomplete) release of insight and that you celebrated with him when he gained the clarity he needed to help his people. I hope that you shared his profound joy as peace was once again restored in his world.

This parable deliberately unfolds in an ancient time, before access to modern neuroscience. This was how early users of the human brain began to explore and understand its complex functionality. Today, under the guidance of cutting-edge technology and research, we can appreciate the biology behind the simple truths the Sage learned on the mountaintop.

Now that you know the Sage's story, I'm going to summarize the parable's underlying scientific principals as we know them today. Our journey into the depths of neuroscience will reveal how our brains are structured and how they function, particularly in response to fear and stress. By understanding the science and applying the principles outlined in this chapter, you will be empowered to master your brain. This mastery is not just an intellectual exercise; it is a path to navigating fear, restoring inner harmony, and achieving a sense of peace and control in your life. The insights you gain here will equip you with practical tools to transform your inner world, which in turn will positively influence your outer reality.

## Fear in Modern Times

To understand the role of fear in our lives, we need to distinguish between fear as experienced by our ancestors and fear as we experience it in our modern world.

The fear-inducing situations our pre-civilization ancestors faced were mainly physical and transient: running to escape and to hunt, or fighting and hiding to protect themselves. Modern humans face a very different stress landscape. Today, most of our stressors are mental or emotional in nature. We seldom need to escape physical threat, chase prey, or fight for survival. It is mainly the anticipation of a potential danger, rather than an actual threat, that triggers our fear response. In addition, we tend to experience modern stressors on a sustained rather than an intermittent basis.

As a result, fear induced by mental or emotional stressors has become a pervasive and contagious force, spreading rapidly across communities and nations. Its spread is accelerated by many factors, including media sensationalism, sociopolitical instability, and the fast pace of technological change. Chronic fear infiltrates our lives through a daily and unbalanced barrage of toxic information, creating an environment wherein anxiety and stress can flourish unchecked.

For us, fear operates much like a virus. It infects individuals, who then spread it to others through their words, actions, and even nonverbal cues. This collective anxiety leads to societal divisions, xenophobia, and widespread unrest. I cannot overstate the urgency to address this modern epidemic of fear. If left unchecked, it will erode the very fabric of our communities, leading to catastrophic breakdown in trust and cooperation. Some might argue that we are already there.

## THE BRAIN OPERATING SYSTEM: OUR KEY TO MASTERING FEAR

Thus, we find ourselves, like the Sage and his villagers, in a precarious position. Society is inflamed. Harmony is not only threatened but becoming elusive. Social disruption spreads rapidly. Our global village is besieged by rampant fear. Like the Sage, we know what we want to achieve but question how to achieve it. To answer this question, we need to understand the biology of the organ where this fear lives, thrives, and expands.

On our journey to understand the intricate workings of the human mind and how it governs our behaviors and emotions, we're going to delve into the scientific foundation of what I call the *Brain Operating System* (BOS). The BOS model provides a framework for understanding how different regions of the brain interact with one another and influence our daily lives. Built on the foundation of the triune (three-part) brain concept originally developed by Paul MacLean,[1] the BOS model incorporates additional brain regions that play vital roles in personal mastery and peak performance.

The human brain, a marvel of evolutionary engineering, has developed over hundreds of millions of years, resulting in a highly sophisticated structure capable of inconceivably complex computational power. But its beginnings were simple.

Approximately 300 million years ago, the earliest reptiles developed a primitive brain (the "reptilian brain") primarily concerned with survival. In evolutionary terms, we humans started with a central brain region that looked and functioned very much like the brains of reptiles and similar cold-blooded animals. Our reptilian brain is our default brain during times of crisis and the seat of our most fundamental survival instincts: fight, flight, or freeze. Governing our behavior with fear and adrenaline, the primitive reptilian brain protects us from immediate danger.

Then, around 200 million years ago, early mammals emerged onto the evolutionary scene with an additional brain region: the limbic system, or "emotional brain." This system enabled these evolved creatures to care for their offspring and collaborate with other adults within their species, enhancing survivability through love and deep social connection. Today, via the emotional brain, we humans can enjoy community and its enormous benefits.

With the advent of primates approximately 50 million years ago, we find the appearance of the neocortex ("cognitive brain"). This brain region introduced advanced thought, reason, and planning and is responsible for memory, strategic computation, and the ability to think abstractly. This giant leap forward conferred huge advantages on us, and the relatively large size of our neocortex versus that of other mammals differentiated the human being from all other animals, enabling us to grapple with and resolve problems way out of reach of other species.

Despite its massive advantages, the arrival of the cognitive brain exposed us to an unexpected risk. We were now able to receive a potentially overwhelming volume of incoming data. The human eyes, for example, are estimated to take in approximately one gigabit ($10^9$ bits) of raw visual data per second.[2] This amounts to a volume of data equivalent to 48 average-length (2.6 MB) e-books entering our brain every second.

To avoid the disastrous results of data overload, Nature created a complex filtering mechanism, which empowered our brains with focus—we could narrow our cognitive power to center on the most important incoming data.

A neural network in the brain stem known as the reticular activating system (RAS) is a key part of this complex filtering mechanism, but neuroscientists now know that other brain components, closely associated with the RAS, are also involved in data filtering. For ease of description, I refer to this system and its collective contributors as the *Attention Focusing Consortium* (AFC). The AFC prevents data overload by prioritizing crucial information and filtering out unhelpful noise.

Millions of years ago, the continued existence of early humans depended on the AFC to filter out less-relevant data to support survival in the wild. Although as modern humans we don't often need to look out for dangerous animals or keep our wits about us when foraging for nonpoisonous plants, we are faced with an even bigger data-overload challenge than that of our ancestors.

The amount of information bombarding our brains daily has increased massively, particularly in relation to the advent and advancement of the digital age and the information era. It's estimated that an amount of information equivalent to that generated between the dawn of human civilization and the year 2003 is currently created every two days.[3] Information overload is a significant stressor in the lives of many people today. Modern humans need the AFC more than ever before to counteract this.

And that's also where the most recent addition to the human brain, the prefrontal cortex, comes in. The prefrontal cortex endows us with self-awareness and higher brain functions, such as judgment and wisdom (sometimes referred to as *metacognition*). It is critical for the mastery of our behaviors and emotions. This most sophisticated gift of Nature—which is a flagship characteristic of the human species and makes us the modern creatures we are today—enables us to have purview over the rest of our brain. Operating from our prefrontal cortex, we are empowered to evaluate and regulate our thoughts, feelings, and fears.

Nature's ingenuity has given us these thoughts, feelings, and fears, the three languages through which our brain communicates with us. Thoughts, feelings, and fears arise from the cognitive, emotional, and reptilian brains, respectively—they are the "voices" of these brain regions. Learning to recognize and distinguish between these three voices is the first step to gaining mastery over fear.

Feeling positive emotions like inner peace, harmony, love, compassion, trust, generosity, and kindness indicates that we're operating from our cognitive and emotional brains because there's a thought behind every positive feeling. In contrast, negative emotions like anger, frustration, hostility, suspicion, intolerance, isolation, and inner pain indicate that the reptilian brain is in control, as every negative feeling originates from a fear.

Another of Nature's smart advances was to ensure that the brain regions have a hierarchy, where higher brain regions (such as the prefrontal cortex) can regulate and override the more primitive ones (such as the reptilian brain). This is possible because, unlike our relationship with the other two brain regions, Nature gave us far-reaching *voluntary* control over our thinking brain. This understanding is crucial for mastering our thoughts, feelings, and fears.

At times of (perceived) crisis, fear takes over. This is a good thing if we are in real danger because the voice of fear initiates our survival instincts, which enable us to react in ways that keep us safe. If, however, we are not in real danger, unregulated fear does not serve us well.

In the absence of regulation by a higher function, the voice of the reptilian brain screams. We hear messages of fear: "Run. Hide. Fight!" And when the reptilian voice of fear shouts the loudest, it overwhelms the quivering emotional brain and evokes negative feelings. We experience anger, frustration, disharmony, suspicion, and doubt. Even though we are not in real danger, we continue to hear the persistent warnings of the reptilian brain, alerting us to all of the potential risks and possible dangers if we fail to protect ourselves from looming threats. This disruptive influence catapults us into discord.

Fortunately, because Nature wired the three brain levels hierarchically, the cognitive brain, together with the emotional brain, can override the compelling, strident, and fearful voice of the reptilian brain—if we instruct it to. When the voice of the cognitive brain dominates, it attracts the attention of the emotional brain, which now exudes positive emotion. When this happens, we amplify feelings of peace, harmony, and compassion and enrich our belief in kindness, cooperation, and collaboration. Messages from the cognitive brain continue to encourage us. The emotional brain magnifies our positive thoughts and propels us forward, urging us to move toward amicable relationships and a life of peace and harmony with others.

Are you starting to see how immensely powerful the human brain is and how knowledge of the BOS and the way the brain regions are designed to work together can bring us to personal mastery of fear?

## The Role of the Cognitive and Emotional Brains in Mastery of Fear

Right now, as you read these words, your emotional brain is actively listening to hear which voice is the loudest—that of positive thoughts (from your cognitive brain) or that of fear (from your reptilian brain). The emotional brain gravitates to the loudest voice. Thought evokes positive feelings; fear evokes negative feelings. For this reason, I call the emotional brain the "great flip flopper."

The boosting capacity of the great flip flopper magnifies enormously the voice that triggers it—for better or for worse. When the voice of the reptilian brain is loudest, the emotional brain responds with a flood of negative emotion; it turboboosts the voice of fear. When the voice of the cognitive brain is loudest, the emotional brain responds with positive emotion; the brain has activated a turbobooster behind the positive thought to drive belief.

We gain mastery over fear when we use our cognitive and emotional brains together to create a belief so powerful it overrides the fear and resistance arising from our reptilian brain.

Interestingly, the emotional brain has another value to me both as coach and as brain user: It is a diagnostic tool that allows us to determine whether thoughts or fears are dominant in our brain at any one moment. When our feelings are negative, we can be sure that our reptilian brain of fear is winning the day. Conversely, when we feel good, we know that thought and reason are prevailing over fear.

When we understand how our brain operates, we can manage our BOS in our favor. We are able to exert voluntary control over an organ that otherwise controls us.

By proactively engaging the executive and cognitive functions of your brain, you can vanquish fear. This process is called *cognitive override*, and you can apply it when it's wise to do so—for example, when a perceived threat is not associated with real danger and arises from a mental or emotional stressor.

Cognitive override involves putting your thinking brain in charge to assess the perceived threat. By doing this, you use your thoughts to gain perspective on the threat and enable you to make the best decisions for how to respond to it. Application of this top-down process makes it possible for you to reconceptualize a fear, thus mitigating its negative effects in your life and the lives of those around you.

The first step in using your BOS to master fear is to shift the seat of your awareness to your prefrontal cortex, and the first action to accomplish this is to simply pause. Taking an intentional pause is fundamental to brain mastery. It's the place you should always start.

Take a few deep breaths. Then, ask and answer: *What am I thinking? What am I feeling? What am I fearing?* When you can answer these three questions, you know you've stepped into the calm space of your prefrontal cortex. Operating from your prefrontal cortex gives you the clarity and perspective to identify and resolve your fears.

Focus on the negative emotions you're experiencing. Probe them to determine any fears under the surface. After you've identified and acknowledged all of your fears, focus on thinking about your situation. Ask yourself questions to discover your thoughts on the matter. For example, What is the real story, unobscured by fears? What might others see or say about your situation from an objective perspective?

As you use your cognitive brain to appraise your situation, you should begin to notice the emergence of positive thoughts. This happens as you begin to naturally rise above the voice of your reptilian brain of fear. Finally, recognize and celebrate the positive feelings you have evoked by thinking—by using your cognitive brain to override fear. Cycle through this process as many times as necessary to achieve positive feelings.

Apply this process whenever you need to override your fears to restore your inner harmony and peace.

## A 7-Step Process to Conquer Fear and Restore Inner Harmony

Though cognitive override, as described above, is an excellent tool when we need to quickly move beyond our fears, we often encounter more stubborn fears that are resistant to simple intervention. Sometimes they are overwhelming in their magnitude and intensity; they're simply too big for a quick fix. Other times, they are deeply entrenched webs that have infiltrated our minds more insidiously; they're too complex for a quick fix.

In these cases, we need a more elaborate and systematic approach to overcoming the fear. Here is a proven 7-step process to accomplish this:

1. **Pause.** Before confronting any fear, take a moment to pause. A pause shifts the seat of your awareness from your reptilian, emotional, and cognitive brains into the calm space of your prefrontal cortex. This grants you immediate access to the executive control necessary to conquer your fear.

2. **Explore.** Once you've shifted your awareness to your prefrontal cortex, you're positioned to examine your fear. Explore the emotions behind the fear you've chosen. Ask yourself: *What am I feeling? What am I fearing?* Then notice the range of emotions you experience as you scrutinize the fear from different angles. Think about descriptive words that best capture your emotions and the sensations you feel in your physical body. Once you've explored your emotions, delve deeper to fully understand the fear: Can you see a link between this fear and other fears you have? What are you actually fearing, deep down? Are there one or more fears hidden behind this one?

3. **Thank.** In this step, you understand and accept that there's an underlying reason for this fear. It has safeguarded you for many years. With genuine

thankfulness, express gratitude for your fear. Recognize the gift this fear has been in your life, and appreciate the positive intentions of your reptilian brain in acting to protect you. When you affirm, acknowledge, express gratitude for, and befriend your fear, it often leads to an aha moment!

4. **Question.** To better understand all angles of your fear, engage in a series of questions. Gather as much data and as many facts as possible. By shedding light on your fear, you unveil inherent flaws in its logic. During this step, it can be helpful to imagine yourself having an amiable, nonjudgmental conversation with yourself, gently probing what your fear is all about. While the specific questions will vary depending on the fear, use the following as a starting point:

- Is this a new fear or one I've had for as long as I can remember?
- Can I pinpoint the origin of this fear?
- Does this fear pertain solely to my life or also to the impact I might have on others?
- In what ways is this fear holding me back?
- In what ways is this fear protecting me?
- Am I afraid of a process or an outcome?
- Is this fear linked to my self-worth, confidence, or competence?
- Is this fear linked to unrealistic expectations I have of myself?
- Am I afraid because of what I've witnessed happening to someone else?
- Is my fear based on other people's opinions of me?
- Am I afraid of losing something or someone precious?
- Am I afraid of having to compel myself to do something I don't want to do?

Select the questions relevant to your fear, or create your own. Questions wield power. They serve as tools to unravel almost any fear, exposing its core.

5. **Interrogate.** Shift from amiable and polite questioning to a more assertive interrogation of your fear. Posture to demonstrate your determination, showing your fear that you mean business and that it has no place to hide. Engage in a firm line of questioning. Demand that it answer:

    - Is this true? Is this *really* true?
    - Is there evidence?
    - How much damage have you (the fear) caused so far?
    - What else are you hiding?
    - What is the accurate probability that there will be irreparable damage?
    - If there is damage, is it true that it couldn't be remedied?

6. **Challenge.** Challenge your fear to prove why you should still listen to its voice. Insist that your fear provide concrete evidence to support its claims; do not back down. Demand answers. Say to your fear, "Justify your argument. Prove you're helping me. Provide hard evidence that substantiates your position." Persist with direct, pointed questions that challenge every claim your reptilian brain shouts.

7. **Disagree.** Claim your victory. Let go of the past, and respectfully disagree with your fear. This is a moment of immense power to relinquish your fear once and for all. You might stand in front of a mirror, look yourself in the eyes, and proclaim (preferably out loud) things like:

    - Respectfully, I disagree.
    - I will no longer heed your arguments.
    - Your voice will not drive my actions.
    - You have yet to consider all the facts. You lack the vision to see the tremendous upside.
    - Respectfully, you're wrong!
    - That's enough. No more shouting.

Depending on the intensity of a particular fear and how long it's been part of your life, conquering it might not require completing all seven steps. Simply understanding the fear through the information gathered during the fourth step—Question—could be enough to reveal it as an overstated force and disempower it.

Conversely, you might need to go through the 7-step process multiple times for intense and deeply rooted fears. You can work through back-to-back iterations in the same session. Sometimes, you may work through the 7-step process and feel frustrated by not conquering the fear immediately. If so, step away. Temporarily ignore the voice of this fear. Engage in activities like exercising, walking in nature, driving, watching a movie, listening to a podcast, or spending time with your family. Tell your fear, "I'm going to step away and ignore you right now, but I'll be back with refreshed energy, new clarity, and more perspective." When you're ready to face the fear once more, begin again.

Each time you work through the 7-step fear-conquering process, celebrate or ritualize your conquest. Celebrating your victory can be as simple as visualizing the disempowered fear in your hand and then releasing it through a window or door, symbolizing its departure from your life.

It takes immense courage to press through and conquer your fears, but now you have the 7-step process to guide you to victory.

## Program Your AFC

Beyond conquering fear through rapid cognitive override or by applying the systematic 7-step process, there are several other BOS practices you can use to master fear.

Another way to use your BOS to master fear is to ensure your AFC is functioning optimally by regularly assessing and adjusting your focus. This involves being mindful of your environment and the fact that you have a filter—which can serve you well or poorly—depending on how you program it. Use your thoughts to focus your attention on what you want or need to see. By doing this, you'll be consciously choosing what information to pay attention to and what to ignore, which enables you to see your actual reality rather than a distorted version of it. A distorted view of reality can spawn irrational fears, which in turn can lead to disharmony and discord.

Every day, you have the opportunity to take voluntary control of your brain to program your AFC to filter in the things you want to see or experience. When you program your AFC accurately to deliver inner harmony and peace, for example, it's like shifting your brain into autopilot. Your well-programmed AFC enables you to navigate your environment subconsciously in a way that automatically leads you to your desired inner state.

A second approach to programming your filter is spot-checking your thoughts. This helps you become aware of whether your thoughts are facts, opinions, or assumptions. In spot-checking thoughts, you're programming your filter by becoming aware of whether you're operating from a basis of fact, opinion, or assumption. This awareness gives you clarity about your situation because opinions and assumptions are potentially harmful distortions that prevent you from seeing your actual reality. For example, if a friend doesn't return a call in a timely fashion, you might feel annoyed with them if you assume that they're ignoring you when, in fact, they're working flat out to complete a work project on a very tight deadline. If you're operating from your assumption, you'll likely feel angry with your friend. However, operating from an understanding of the fact that they're under extreme work pressure is likely to elicit feelings of compassion from you.

You can also use Socratic questioning to challenge the accuracy of what you think about yourself and your life experiences using thoughtful questions to prompt deep reflection and honest inquiry. The benefit of this method is that it challenges the accuracy of what you think about yourself and your life experiences objectively, systematically, and thoroughly. Ask yourself questions like: Could I be jumping to conclusions? Am I considering all the evidence, or could I be missing something important or misinterpreting the evidence I am seeing? Am I blaming myself for a situation that involves many factors that are out of my control? Could I be demanding something of myself that is unrealistic or holding myself responsible for something that someone else should be doing?

Finally, you can program your filter via calibration. This involves seeking input and feedback from others to broaden your perspective and to confirm that your interpretations are accurate and not distorted by fears. Calibration is a valuable tool to use when you're feeling overwhelmed by your fears, or at risk of overlooking essential details, or struggling to see the full range of options and possibilities that are available to you. You can't see everything, but your friends and family have the benefit of an external vantage point. Their unique perspectives, experiences, and viewpoints can help you resolve difficult situations with great objectivity and avoid dangerous pitfalls and blind spots. You'll have the clarity to move forward and make more informed decisions based on a comprehensive understanding of the facts, rather than from a limited, fear-based perspective of your situation.

## DRIVE BELIEF

To drive belief in your ability to attain and maintain inner harmony and peace, you need to use Nature's gift of voluntary control over your cognitive brain. There are a number strategies you can implement to achieve this.

To maximize cognitive override, foster positive thoughts so that the voice of your cognitive brain shouts the loudest. Regularly visualize positive outcomes to strengthen your belief in your capabilities. This helps to silence the voice of fear and reinforce a positive mental state.

We all have particular strengths, abilities, and attributes that benefit ourselves and those around us—these are our personal assets. You can boost your belief and amplify your self-confidence by focusing on your top three personal assets. Positive thoughts about your personal assets originate in your cognitive brain, so when you think about your top assets, you take voluntary control of your brain—quickly, easily, and automatically. You can instantly replace negative thoughts with positive ones just by seeing yourself in a positive light.

An active gratitude practice also builds belief. Practicing gratitude on a regular basis fills your brain with positivity. By recognizing, acknowledging, and appreciating the good—whether or not it's related to your current situation—you're enabling yourself to use the power of choice to transform bad into good and good into best.

Reciting mantras gives you a structured way of immediately taking control of your thoughts to consciously focus on what you want, especially when the voice of your reptilian brain is strident. Mantras are short, self-affirming, and empowering thoughts that contain positive words or phrases. They concisely express the way you want your life to be. A mantra gives you a positive thought to latch onto and, when repeated silently or out loud, can shift your brain from a fear-based focus to positivity.

The way you hold or move your body can also power up positivity and drive belief. Use power poses or occupy space when you move to elevate your self-confidence, reduce your fear and nervousness, drive feelings of power, and evoke happiness and optimism. Power poses are expansive postures characterized by sitting or standing tall with one's head held high, shoulders back, and hands on hips or one or both arms raised. Power movements include walking in a way that you carry yourself with positive energy and pride. Together, your cognitive brain and expansive body postures or movements can override fear and drive positivity.

## Activate Desire

Activating desire involves systematically accentuating the voice of the emotional brain to boost belief and positivity. Activating desire results from a combination of cognition and emotion. Whatever you choose to do, it's important to prioritize cognition as the starting point. Then, do anything and everything you can to enhance the power of your emotional brain to support your positive thoughts. Together, the voices of the cognitive and emotional brains can override the voice of fear, making inner harmony and peace possible.

To activate desire, engage your emotional brain by cultivating strong, positive emotions about your goals. This can be achieved through practices such as gratitude journaling, meditation, and building strong social connections that support and motivate you.

Expanding your emotional vocabulary (the words you use to describe your emotions) gives you the ability to activate your emotional brain more fully. As you expand your emotional vocabulary, you activate desire and override fear. To expand your emotional vocabulary, pay attention to the emotion words you use most often and actively think about other, more nuanced emotion words you could use to describe your emotions (or the emotions of others). For example, imagine yourself experiencing inner harmony and think about other words you could use to describe what you're feeling. Words that describe emotions associated with inner harmony include *contentment, tranquility, happiness,* and *serenity.* Expanding your emotional vocabulary can also help you to improve your communication skills in your professional and personal relationships by enabling you to better understand your emotions and the emotions of others as well as to express your needs more specifically.

The senses—hearing, touch, smell, taste, and sight—evoke positive emotions quickly and powerfully. You can use sensory prompts in your day-to-day life to activate desire and keep fear at bay. There are many ways to use the senses to evoke positive emotions, but the easiest and most powerful one is to use your sense of hearing to evoke the emotion you want, when you want it by listening to a song that reflects the emotion you choose to feel.

By understanding the intricate workings of your BOS and applying the practices I have described above, you can master your brain's functioning. This mastery allows you to navigate fear, harness the power of positive thoughts and emotions, and ultimately achieve inner harmony and peace in your life, and collaboration and cooperation with those around you.

## CHAPTER 3
# THE ACTION

The strife in our world today is *real*. From the exchange of harsh words between family members to the large-scale expressions of enmity that threaten world peace, the troubles afflicting our world must be taken seriously.

We live in an age of enormous individual psychological complexity and vast social, cultural, economic, and political intrigue. Crisis seems constant and conflict seems unavoidable. It is all too easy for fear to dominate under these conditions, making peace feel increasingly elusive.

The solution to this global crisis starts individually. If each of us adopts the simple approach outlined in this book to maintaining our own mental and emotional hygiene, and if each of us commits to mastering fear to restore inner harmony, then each life, family, home, city, country, and continent will be in a better place.

## Healing a Fear-Full World

Our village is the community we live in, including our family, our workplace, and our neighborhood. We are all part of village life; thus, we all contribute to the peace and harmony—or lack thereof—in our own village.

This parable illustrates the contrast between peace-full and fear-full village life. It is not difficult to see which state most closely parallels the world we live in today. With massive polarization, suspicion, paranoia, and hostile conflict the norm, it is abundantly evident that we inhabit a world where fear rules unchecked and suffering ensues.

Some may feel that our human frailty is such that disharmony, discord, and strife are inevitable and that the vision of peace, tranquility, and harmony at every level of society is a dream beyond our reach. They will argue that this parable is simply a utopian tale with an unrealistic happily-ever-after ending.

Their argument would be correct if we were not neurobiologically equipped with the means to master fear. But the fact is that we *do* have our BOS, and we *can* master it. We *can* attain peace and harmony both individually and collectively.

The threat of danger and the fear-driven suffering that is currently endemic in every heart and in every home is avoidable. Each of us carries within us a wellspring of wisdom, resilience, and compassion. By understanding and managing our own BOS, we can liberate ourselves from the chains that hold us back, finding peace and strength in even these most turbulent times.

The Sage in the parable represents each of us. With the conviction that there is a better way to live, I invite you to travel through the intricate workings of your mind to find answers. Journeying alongside the Sage, you will discover, explore, understand, and finally master your BOS. I invite you to dismantle the negative impact of fear-based living using the tools I have provided in this book.

Once you have mastered your own fear, I invite you to return triumphant to your village, inspiring similar efforts in your family and friends. If you and every other "villager" commits to mastering their fear, then peace and harmony will prevail. Similarly, as each village masters fear, then peace and harmony will spread from county to country to continent, and beyond.

This is the urgent call to real action.

Personal transformation is the first ripple in a wave that can spread far and wide. As you harness the power of your BOS and restore your inner harmony, you become a living example of what's possible. Your calm, centered presence will naturally influence those around you, fostering a culture of understanding and cooperation.

This doesn't happen overnight. The process requires courage and commitment, much like the Sage's arduous ascent to the mountaintop.

## Your Journey Is Just Beginning

Your journey doesn't end here, in this final chapter; it's only just beginning. I invite you to continue your exploration and growth by visiting my website, www.roddycarter.com, where you'll find a wealth of resources, courses, and services designed to support your ongoing development. Engage with the community, join programs, and access tools that will help you deepen your understanding and mastery of your BOS.

The Roddy Carter community is a vibrant group of caring and hardworking leaders who are dedicated to applying scientific strategies to uplift their own lives and their communities. Together, we share experiences, inspire each other, and work toward creating a world grounded in compassion, understanding, and harmony. Your participation in this community is not just an opportunity for personal growth but a chance to contribute to a collective journey of transformation. Stay in touch, share your stories, and let us continue to embolden one another on this remarkable path.

The sources of BOS wisdom are myriad. I encourage you to read widely, and to listen to other scientists who practice in this field. You will find many interesting resources in the final section of this book. Experiment with their techniques. Practice, practice, and practice some more. Return to the mountaintop often to revisit the BOS wisdom. On refreshing and deepening your knowledge, apply it earnestly to enhance your inner and outer worlds.

The wisdom gained from this journey is not meant to be hoarded but shared. By spreading enlightenment, we will help others navigate their fears and restore balance in their own lives. This collective awakening will lead to a healthier and more harmonious society where fear no longer dictates our actions and decisions or threatens our global survival.

The missive is clear: Personal mastery over fear is the key to societal transformation. When we ignite peace within our individual spaces, we create a foundation for cooperation and collaboration that radiates by contiguous flow to infuse and transform the entire world.

Thank you for joining me on this journey. Let's continue to walk this path together, hand in hand, heart to heart, transforming our lives and our world one step at a time. When we tame the serpent within, we each play a meaningful role in bringing peace and joy to the world.

---

If this book resonated with you, I'd be honored if you'd leave a review on the site where you purchased it...your voice helps others find it.

# ADDITIONAL READING

Should you wish to delve into some of the research that supports the BOS principles and practices discussed in this book, I invite you to explore the resources provided below.

## THE FIVE-REGION BOS MODEL

The BOS model is an adaptation of the triune brain concept developed by Paul MacLean, an American physician and neuroscientist. MacLean developed this concept to provide a neurobiological and neuroevolutionary explanation of human psychology and behavior; he wanted to answer profound questions about the human brain-behavior link. MacLean conceptualized his triune brain concept based on extensive research and published it in detail in a 1990 book titled *The Triune Brain in Evolution: Role in Paleocerebral Functions*. In the BOS model, the brain regions referred to as the "reptilian," "emotional," and "cognitive" brains are based on MacLean's triune brain concept.

The other two BOS components, the prefrontal cortex and the AFC, were added to incorporate the important roles these brain regions play in the attainment of personal mastery. There is much published research about the structure and function of the prefrontal cortex and the AFC, and about their influence on behavior. Two such articles are listed below:

- Alves, P. N., Forkel, S. J., Corbetta, M., & Thiebaut de Schotten, M. (2022). The subcortical and neurochemical organization of the ventral and dorsal attention networks. *Communication Biology, 5*, 1343. https://doi.org/10.1038/s42003-022-04281-0
- Dahl, C. J., Wilson-Mendenhall, C. D., & Davidson, R. J. (2020). The plasticity of well-being: A training-based framework for the cultivation of human flourishing. *Proceedings of the National Academy of Sciences, 117*(51), 32197–32206. https://doi.org/10.1073/pnas.2014859117

## Cognitive Override

As discussed in Chapter 2, the brain's hierarchical structure enables voluntary control of emotions. This means that, by choice, cognition can be used to override fear. This process is referred to as the *top-down regulation of emotions*.

The brain circuitry design that facilitates executive and cognitive emotion regulation and fear override is reflected in a large body of scientific research published over the past few decades and is empirically supported by behavioral observation. If you're interested in learning more about this magnificent biology and the simple model used to represent it, you can read more about the science in the following articles:

- Diekhof, E. K., Geier, K., Falkaj, P., & Gruber, O. (2011). Fear is only as deep as the mind allows: A coordinate-based meta-analysis of neuroimaging studies on the regulation of negative affect. *Neuroimage, 58*(1), 275–285. https://doi.org/10.1016/j.neuroimage.2011.05.073
- Etkin, A., Büchel, C., & Gross, J. J. (2015). The neural bases of emotion regulation. *Nature Reviews Neuroscience, 16*(11), 693–700. https://doi.org/10.1038/nrn4044
- Hariri, A. R., Bookheimer, S. Y., & Mazziotta, J. C. (2000). Modulating emotional responses: Effects of a neocortical network on the limbic system. *NeuroReport, 11*(1), 43–48. https://10.1097/00001756-200001170-00009
- Javanbakht, A., & Saab, L. (2017). The science of fright: Why we love to be scared. *The Conversation.* https://theconversation.com/the-science-of-fright-why-we-love-to-be-scared-85885
- Ochsner, K. N., & Gross, J. J. (2005). The cognitive control of emotion. *Trends in Cognitive Sciences, 9*(5), 242–249. https://doi.org/10.1016/j.tics.2005.03.010
- Ochsner, K. N., Silvers, J. A., & Buhle, J. T. (2012). Functional imaging studies of emotion regulation: A synthetic review and evolving model of the cognitive control of emotion. *Annals of the New York Academy of Sciences, 1251*(1), E1–E24. https://pmc.ncbi.nlm.nih.gov/articles/PMC4133790/

- Öner, S. (2018). Neural substrates of cognitive emotion regulation: A brief review. *Psychiatry and Clinical Psychopharmacology, 28*(1), 91–96. https://doi.org/10.1080/24750573.2017.1407563

## Visualization

Chapter 2 includes a discussion of select strategies that will assist you in taking voluntary control of your cognitive brain to drive belief and activate desire, but there are many more. I outline several of these additional strategies below, followed by articles that explore the scientific evidence supporting the efficacy of these strategies.

The first, visualization, the use of mental imagery, is known to be an effective technique for positively influencing thoughts, emotions, and behaviors. Imagining desired scenarios and outcomes can help with emotional regulation by increasing optimism and positivity. Visualization can also be used to assist with decision-making, problem-solving, planning, and motivation. Explore the following articles to learn more about the benefits of using visualization to enhance positivity and happiness:

- Meevissen, Y. M. C., Peters, M. L., & Alberts, H. J. E. M. (2011). Become more optimistic by imagining a best possible self: Effects of a two week intervention. *Journal of Behavior Therapy and Experimental Psychiatry, 42*(3), 371–378. https://doi.org/10.1016/j.jbtep.2011.02.012
- Renner, F., Murphy, F. C., Ji, J. L., Manly, T., & Holmes, E. A. (2019). Mental imagery as a "motivational amplifier" to promote activities. *Behaviour Research and Therapy, 114*, 51–59. https://doi.org/10.1016/j.brat.2019.02.002
- Schubert, T., Eloo, R., Scharfen, J., & Morina, N. (2020). How imagining personal future scenarios influences affect: Systematic review and meta-analysis. *Clinical Psychology Review, 75*, 101811. https://doi.org/10.1016/j.cpr.2019.101811
- Spreng, R. N., & Levine, B. (2013). Doing what we imagine: Completion rates and frequency attributes of imagined future events one year after prospection. *Memory, 21*(4), 458–466. https://doi.org/10.1080/09658211.2012.736524

## Gratitude

There are a number of excellent articles on the functions and benefits of gratitude. A selection of these articles is provided below:

- Algoa, S. B. (2012). Find, remind, and bind: The functions of gratitude in everyday relationships. *Social and Personality Psychology Compass, 6*(6), 455–469. https://doi.org/10.1111/j.1751-9004.2012.00439.x
- Di Fabio, A., Palazzeschi, L., & Bucci, O. (2017). Gratitude in organizations: A contribution for healthy organizational contexts. *Frontiers in Psychology, 8*(2025). https://doi.org/10.3389/fpsyg.2017.02025
- Diniz, G., Korkes, L., Tristão, L. S., Pelegrini, R., Bellodi, P. L., & Bernardo, W. M. (2023). The effects of gratitude interventions: A systematic review and meta-analysis. *Einstein (São Paulo), 21*, eRW0371. https://pmc.ncbi.nlm.nih.gov/articles/PMC10393216/
- Giacomo, B., & Jason, T. S. (2018). How gratitude connects humans to the best in themselves and in others. *Research in Human Development, 15*(3-4), 224–237. https://doi.org/10.1080/15427609.2018.1499350
- Jans-Beken, L., Jacobs, N., Janssens, M., Peeters, S., Reijnders, J., Lechner, L., & Lataster, J. (2020). Gratitude and health: An updated review. *The Journal of Positive Psychology, 15*(6), 743–782. https://doi.org/10.1080/17439760.2019.1651888
- Kirca, A., Malouff, J. M., & Meynadier, J. (2023). The effect of expressed gratitude interventions on psychological wellbeing: A meta-analysis of randomised controlled studies. *International Journal of Applied Positive Psychology, 8*(1), 63–86. https://doi.org/10.1007/s41042-023-00086-6
- Nelson, C. (2009). Appreciating gratitude: Can gratitude be used as a psychological intervention to improve individual well-being? *Counselling Psychology Review, 24*(3-4), 38–50. https://doi.org/10.53841/bpscpr.2009.24.3-4.38
- Wood, A. M., Froh, J. J., & Geraghty, A. W. A. (2010). Gratitude and well-being: A review and theoretical integration. *Clinical Psychology Review, 30*(7), 890–905. https://doi.org/10.1016/j.cpr.2010.03.005
- Yoshimura, S. M., & Berzins, K. (2017). Grateful experiences and expressions: The role of gratitude expressions in the link between gratitude experiences and well-being. *Review of Communications, 17*(2), 106–118. https://doi.org/10.1080/15358593.2017.1293836

## Power Postures and Movements

There is a direct link between your body and your brain. When your brain alone isn't enough, you can override fear and drive positivity by using expansive body postures or movements. Explore the following resources to learn more:

- Cuddy, A. J. C. (2018). Presence: Bringing your boldest self to your biggest challenges. *IDEAcademy 2018 presentation*. https://youtu.be/ATo9sYax-AQ?si=laH3CnfSzyChiupn (Video: 1:08:28).
- Lanke, P., & Nath, P. (2023). The relationship between dance and well-being: Examining the underlying mechanism and outcomes. *World Leisure Journal*, 66(1), 134–150. https://doi.org/10.1080/16078055.2023.2243249
- Nair, S., Sagar, M., Sollers, J. III, Consedine, N., & Broadbent, E. (2015). Do slumped and upright postures affect stress responses? A randomized trial. *Health Psychology*, 34(6), 632–641. https://doi.org/10.1037/hea0000146
- Shafir, T. (2016). Using movement to regulate emotion: Neurophysiological findings and their application in psychotherapy. *Frontiers in Psychology*, 7(1451). https://doi.org/10.3389/fpsyg.2016.01451
- Shafir, T., Tsachor, R. P., & Welch, K. B. (2016). Emotion regulation through movement: Unique sets of movement characteristics are associated with and enhance basic emotions. *Frontiers in Psychology*, 6(2030). https://doi.org/10.3389/fpsyg.2015.02030
- Takayama, A., & Sekiya, H. (2023). Effects of various sitting and standing postures on arousal and valence. *PLoS ONE*, 18(6), e0286720. https://doi.org/10.1371/journal.pone.0286720
- Van Geest, J., Samaritter, R., & van Hooren, S. (2021). Move and be moved: The effect of moving specific movement elements on the experience of happiness. *Frontiers in Psychology*, 11(579518). https://doi.org/10.3389/fpsyg.2020.579518

## Emotional Vocabulary in Expressive Writing

Expressive writing (including journaling) as a cognitive practice has been researched for its positive impact on emotional well-being. It facilitates self-reflection and awareness and acknowledgement of emotions, which can lead to emotional regulation. The following articles provide more information:

- Baikie, K., & Wilhelm, K. (2005). Emotional and physical health benefits of expressive writing. *Advances in Psychiatric Treatment, 11*(5), 338–346. https://doi.org/10.1192/apt.11.5.338

- Harrist, S., Carlozzi, B. L., McGovern, A. R., & Harrist, A. W. (2007). Benefits of expressive writing and expressive talking about life goals. *Journal of Research in Personality, 41*(4), 923–930. https://doi.org/10.1016/j.jrp.2006.09.002

- Lepore, S. J., Greenberg, M. A., Bruno, M., & Smyth, J. M. (2002). Expressive writing and health: Self-regulation of emotion-related experience, physiology, and behavior. In S. J. Lepore & J. M. Smyth (Eds.), *The writing cure: How expressive writing promotes health and emotional well-being* (pp. 99–117). American Psychological Association.

- Pennebaker, J. W., & Chung, C. K. (2011). Expressive writing: Connections to physical and mental health. In H. S. Friedman (Ed.), *The Oxford handbook of health psychology* (pp. 417–437). Oxford University Press.

- Ruini, C., & Mortara, C. C. (2022). Writing technique across psychotherapies—from traditional expressive writing to new positive psychology interventions: A narrative review. *Journal of Contemporary Psychotherapy, 52*, 23–34. https://doi.org/10.1007/s10879-021-09520-9

## Music

There is a strong link between music and emotion. This facilitates the use of music in research on emotions and the brain; for example, music can be used to evoke particular emotions and the brain activity associated with these emotions can be recorded using functional magnetic resonance imaging (fMRI). This helps with elucidating emotion circuits. Because music modulates activity in the emotion circuits, it can be used effectively to regulate emotion. Explore the following articles to find out more about music and the brain:

- Blasco-Magraner, J. S., Bernabé-Valero, G., Marín-Liébana, P., & Botella-Nicolas, A. M. (2023). Changing positive and negative affects through music experiences: A study with university students. *BMC Psychology, 11*, 76. https://doi.org/10.1186/s40359-023-01110-9

- Cook, T., Roy, A. R. K., & Welker, K. M. (2019). Music as an emotion regulation strategy: An examination of genres of music and their roles in emotion regulation. *Psychology of Music, 47*(1), 144–154. https://doi.org/10.1177/0305735617734627
- Koelsch, S. (2014). Brain correlates of music-evoked emotions. *Nature Reviews Neuroscience, 15,* 170–180. https://doi.org/10.1038/nrn3666
- Trost, W., Ethofer, T., Zentner, M., & Vuilleumier, P. (2012). Mapping aesthetic musical emotions in the brain. *Cerebral Cortex, 22*(12), 2769–2783. https://doi.org/10.1093/cercor/bhr353

## Mindfulness Practices

Mindfulness practices are known to have positive benefits on emotional and psychological well-being, including reducing and managing stress, improving cognition, and allowing for more effective emotion regulation. The following articles speak to the benefits of mindfulness on emotional well-being:

- Compare, A., Zarbo, C., Shonin, E., Van Gordon, W., & Marconi, C. (2014). Emotional regulation and depression: A potential mediator between heart and mind. *Cardiovascular Psychiatry and Neurology, 2014,* 324374. https://doi.org/10.1155/2014/324374
- Djernis, D., Lundsgaard, C. M., Rønn-Smidt, H., & Dahlgaard, J. (2023). Nature-based mindfulness: A qualitative study of the experience of support for self-regulation. *Healthcare, 11*(6), 905. https://doi.org/10.3390/healthcare11060905
- Garland, E., Gaylord, S., & Park, J. (2009). The role of mindfulness in positive reappraisal. *EXPLORE, 5*(1), 37–44. https://doi.org/10.1016/j.explore.2008.10.001
- Grecucci, A., Pappaianni, E., Siugzdaite, R. Theuninck, A., & Job, R. (2015). Mindful emotion regulation: Exploring the neurocognitive mechanism behind mindfulness. *BioMed Research International, 2015,* 670724. https://doi.org/10.1155/2015/670724
- Herwig, U., Kaffenberger, T., Jäncke, L., & Brühl, A. B. (2010). Self-related awareness and emotion regulation. *NeuroImage, 50*(2), 734–741. https://doi.org/10.1016/j.neuroimage.2009.12.089
- Hölzel, B. K., Carmody, J., Vangel, M., Congleton, C., Yerramsetti, S. M., Gard, T., & Lazar, S. W. (2011). Mindfulness practice leads to increases

in regional brain gray matter density. *Psychiatry Research: Neuroimaging, 19*(1), 36–43. https://doi.org/10.1016/j.pscychresns.2010.08.006

- Lutz, J., Herwig, U., Opialla, S., Hittmeyer, A., Jäncke, L., Rufer, M., Holtforth, M. G., & Brühl, A. B. (2014). Mindfulness and emotion regulation—an fMRI study. *Social Cognitive and Affective Neuroscience, 9*(6), 776–785. https://doi.org/10.1093/scan/nst043

- Schuman-Olivier, Z., Trombka, M., Lovas, D. A., Brewer, J. A., Vago, D. R., Gawande, R., Dunne, J. P., Lazar, S. W., Loucks, E. B., & Fulwiler, C. (2020). Mindfulness and behavior change. *Harvard Review of Psychiatry, 28*(6), 371–394. https://doi.org/10.1097/HRP.0000000000000277

- Schutte, N. S., & Malouff, J. M. (2011). Emotional intelligence mediates the relationship between mindfulness and subjective well-being. *Personality and Individual Differences, 50*(7), 1116–1119. https://doi.org/10.1016/j.paid.2011.01.037

## DEEP BREATHING AND THE MASTERY OF FEAR

The autonomic nervous system, composed of the sympathetic and parasympathetic nervous systems, regulates vital physiological processes. It operates automatically, outside of voluntary control, but it can be influenced indirectly using breathing techniques. Intentional slow, deep breathing can be used to purposefully activate the parasympathetic ("rest-and-digest") nervous system and deactivate the sympathetic ("fight-or-flight") nervous system.

Breath control is a powerful way to manage stress. This is possible because breathing and stress are linked. When stress levels are high, chest breathing dominates. But the impact of stress can be countered by enforcing a pattern of slow, deep abdominal breathing. Voluntary, controlled breathing interventions enable a shift of unhealthy physiological responses toward more balanced, positive ones. Controlled breathing is especially effective in situations that are stressful but not life threatening.

Proactively shifting to the parasympathetic state not only calms the body but also calms the brain to support clear, conscious, mindful execution of cognitive control. Research shows a positive association between the calm, relaxed parasympathetic state and prefrontal cortex executive function, goal-directed behavior, and emotional regulation.

Additional Reading

Explore the following articles to learn more about the benefits of deep breathing:

- De Couck, M., Caers, R., Musch, L., Fliegauf, J., Giangreco, A., & Gidron, Y. (2019). How breathing can help you make better decisions: Two studies on the effects of breathing patterns on heart rate variability and decision-making in business cases. *International Journal of Psychophysiology, 139*, 1–9. https://doi.org/10.1016/j.ijpsycho.2019.02.011
- Gerritsen, R. J. S., & Band, G. P. H. (2018). Breath of life: The respiratory vagal stimulation model of contemplative activity. *Frontiers in Human Neuroscience, 12*, 397. https://doi.org/10.3389/fnhum.2018.00397
- Hopper, S. I., Murray, S. L., Ferrara, L. R., & Singleton, J. K. (2019). Effectiveness of diaphragmatic breathing for reducing physiological and psychological stress in adults: A quantitative systematic review. *JBI Database of Systematic Reviews and Implementation Reports, 17*(9). 1855–1876. https://pubmed.ncbi.nlm.nih.gov/31436595/
- Ma, X., Yue, Z.-Q., Gong, Z.-Q., Zhang, H., Duan, N.-Y., Shi, Y.-T., Wei, G. X., & Li, Y. F. (2017). The effects of diaphragmatic breathing on attention, negative affect and stress in healthy adults. *Frontiers in Psychology, 8*(874). https://doi.org/10.3389/fpsyg.2017.00874
- Zaccaro, A., Piarulli, A., Laurino, M., Garbella, E., Menicucci, D., Neri, B., & Gemignani, A. (2018). How breath-control can change your life: A systematic review on psycho-physiological correlates of slow breathing. *Frontiers in Human Neuroscience, 12*, 353. https://doi.org/10.3389/fnhum.2018.00353

# NOTES

1. MacLean, P. D. (1990). *The triune brain in evolution: Role in paleocerebral functions*. Plenum Press.

2. Lee, K. H., Tran, A., Turan, Z., & Meister, M. (2020). The sifting of visual information in the superior colliculus. *eLife, 9*, e50678. https://doi.org/10.7554/eLife.50678

3. Arnold, M., Goldschmitt, M., & Rigotti, T. (2023). Dealing with information overload: A comprehensive review. *Frontiers in Psychology, 14*, 1122200. https://doi.org/10.3389/fpsyg.2023.1122200

www.ingramcontent.com/pod-product-compliance
Lightning Source LLC
Chambersburg PA
CBHW040234110526
44582CB00002B/56